Mental Health
&
Stress

Mental Health
&
Stress

Wellness Solutions Before A Crisis

MARISSA YOUNG

authorHOUSE®

AuthorHouse™
1663 Liberty Drive
Bloomington, IN 47403
www.authorhouse.com
Phone: 1-800-839-8640

Published by AuthorHouse   10/17/2012

ISBN: 978-1-4772-7469-9 (sc)
ISBN: 978-1-4772-7468-2 (e)

Library of Congress Control Number: 2012917918

This book is dedicated to my beloved mom and dad as well as my brother, doctors, counsellors, nurses, therapists, pastors and friends. Last but not the least, I thank the Lord my God for giving me the inspiration to writing this book.

CONTENTS

ACKNOWLEDGMENTS

Before I embark on my story, I have to emphasize that there have been changes made to all the names of actual people who have helped me in the past and present, including my parents, friends, and community support workers.

I would like to express my utmost gratitude to my parents, who have instilled in me many positive values, morals, and disciplines over the years. Mom and Dad, you have been very patient with me throughout my mood swings. Despite your own difficulties, you have supported me emotionally and financially. Without your love and support, I would not be what I am today: strong and determined as ever to view struggles as positive challenges that help me to better myself in the long run.

I thank all my psychiatrists who have worked with me in my diagnosis and control of my ailment. To my community support workers—words are not enough to express my gratitude to you for your love, care, and concern for me, and most of all for believing in me. Thank you to all my "prayer warriors" who choose to remain unknown, for all the immeasurable things they have done for me. I wish to extend my thanks to my case managers at a mental health association, and my therapists and nurses in all the hospitals I have been through—especially the nurses, psychotherapists, occupational therapists, and case workers at the Day Clinics within the hospitals who have encouraged me to think positive and move on. Last but not least, thanks to my pastors, relatives, and friends for being very supportive of me during my ups and downs.

CHAPTER 1

Diagnosis

In 1988, I graduated with an Ordinary degree in Linguistics from a university in Canada. Around the same time, a friend of mine, Edward, who had been blind since birth, seriously mentioned that he sensed a dark aura around me. I took his comments lightly, but as it turned out, darkness was indeed closing in.

I had decided to visit my parents in Singapore for two months before heading back to Canada to continue with a Double Major Honours degree. I did not foresee what was ahead of me. When the plane touched down, I felt glad to be home. However, the weather was extremely humid, and that made me very irritable.

For most of my visit, my parents struggled to accept the fact that I had converted from a Catholic to a Protestant. They also disapproved of the fact that I did not want to live in my old hometown anymore, as I had become accustomed to the easygoing Canadian lifestyle. My parents took it that I was not filial toward them. They were hurt that I had chosen to abandon them. Due to the constant shouting matches, I did not get a chance to give them the whole story—that I wanted them to live with me in Canada too! In my culture, children are to respect their elders, with no question at all. I started wondering about myself: why this sudden change? Being disrespectful toward my parents was not part of who I was, but suddenly, I could not control my anger. Soon, both sides refused to hear the other. It became a lose-lose situation.

After the two-month visit, I returned to Canada. I could not sleep for two weeks, as I felt void of parental love. I was crying constantly and felt suicidal. During that time, I stayed on campus at the university. I noticed that a couple in another dorm were burning incense and were intrigued by the notion of death. I tried to talk them into pushing me off a cliff. They refused. Then I started voicing my suicidal thoughts to another friend. I mentioned to her that my visit with my parents had left me feeling very empty inside. She quickly alerted the supervisor of the campus, who happened to be a psychotherapist. It was then that I started seeing a psychiatrist.

During my first visit with the doctor, he diagnosed me as Manic Depressive or Bipolar Type 1 (where one's mood goes up and down uncontrollably). During my first bout of depression, I could not see the light at the end of the tunnel. I would ask myself when my depression would end. When would I be "normal" again? It was a complete sense of helplessness and hopelessness. At that particular time, I suffered memory loss, was unable to concentrate on my studies, and lost half a year of university in my fourth year. I could not understand what I was reading. Whatever was on the television, I was not able to focus on. I was feeling fatigued and overwhelmed all the time. Nothing could cheer me up, not even the presence and comfort of my mother, who came to visit me a couple of months later after my aunt mentioned my sickness to her. For the next six months, I would say to myself, "Just when I will be useful again?"

I was forced to take medication for my depression. Only after trying out a whole series of pills on me, my psychiatrist and I settled with a combination of drugs named: Lithium (a mood stabilizer), Paxil, and Imovane. In the beginning, I thought I was being treated like a guinea pig. However, I know now that the right combination of drugs is prescribed based on trial and error. Every individual is unique, and not everyone has the same positive results with the pills that I take.

In 1990, I graduated with a Double Major Honours degree in Mass Communication and Linguistics. I had regained my ability to study because the right combination of pills had stabilized my mood swings. Pills, however, were not the only solution. One of my successes in the control of my mood swings was my determination to cooperate with my doctor's advice at that point in time. He mentioned to me that I must never go off the pills on my own, without supervision. He provided me with counselling and hypnosis as well.

Time was also a healing factor. I had taken a year off from studying. I didn't know how long it was going to take to get on the road to recovery. Bear in mind, getting better differs for each individual. For me, a combination of faith in God, courage from within, and the encouragement from my doctor, counsellor, and mom and dad all worked to lead me to my quick recovery.

I also charted my sleeping patterns, indicating the time when I fell asleep and the time I woke up. For me, the best is at least eight hours. Sleeping patterns vary for different individuals. Getting the proper sleep is extremely important. If you cannot sleep for a week, you must seek help. Lack of sleep can lead to irritability, anger problems, and eventually stress that you cannot handle anymore. This is a trick you need to know about: a good sleeping pattern will prevent a crisis of any kind. If there is a complete lack of sleep, stress will definitely come down hard. Things will start to spiral downhill and lead to depression. On the other hand, if you are too depressed, you may sleep too much. This is why it is very important to realize the signs and symptoms of your own mental health.

CHAPTER 2

Hallucinations

In 1993, I was doing so well, I felt that I could do without the pills. Friends were starting to discourage me from using the medication. They said it was all in my mind. I gradually missed doses in the end of 1993. I still did not understand the true meaning of being Bipolar. I thought it was just depression. But as I went off the medication, things started to change for the worse. My anger came back. At one point, I yelled at a colleague with words that were quite atrocious, as I felt that he was sexually harassing me. I was let go from my job, even though the manager—who regarded me as a conscientious and pleasant worker—found it a difficult decision. I was glad in later years that my manager did not hold any grudges against me. He had always admired my work and dedication.

Around the same time, my personal relationships went downhill thanks to my uncalled-for behaviour of suspiciousness and rage. In mid-1994, I had an attack of mania, because I had decided to go off the pills by myself in a gradual way. I didn't realize I was getting sick again. Hallucinations became a part of my everyday life. One day, as I was on Highway 401, I saw visions of cars driving backward and all over the place. I was seeing things that were not there. I exited from the highway and headed to pick up Edward at the university campus where he was staying for a short while. I mentioned to him my visual "encounters." We soon drifted off to other topics, and I did not think much of my brief visual hallucination. My hearing was heightened as well; I could hear everything very loudly. I started laughing and giggling a lot—it was a feeling of euphoria. I had a great two weeks with Edward, driving him everywhere. We still did not suspect that anything was wrong with me.

Soon, I became extremely religious. I heard a voice telling me that I was the Christ, and I started preaching the Gospel to the public at a grocery store across from my residence. I saw that the lottery tickets were sold in the supermarket, and I threw them down, thinking how angry Jesus was (in the Bible) when he saw people gambling in his temple two thousand years ago. My mind was just weaving in and out between a dream and reality. I started "seeing" people who were "crippled" and started "healing" them, as I thought that I was the Christ. I was seeing things that were not real and hearing voices.

Mom came to visit my brother and I in 1994; we were living in the same condominium at that time. The two of them watched in horror what was happening to me each day. I remembered on a Good Friday, I went to seek out a medical doctor by the name of Dr. Luke—and I found him! I suspected him to be one of the apostles in the Bible named Luke, of whom I thought was a doctor during the biblical times two thousand years ago. I believe that I mentioned to his secretary that the doctor could perform miracles, as he was one of Jesus's apostles. There was confusion in my thinking. I became psychotic without knowing it.

I know that the term *psychotic* will be a red flag to many reading my book. Psychosis occurs when one is hallucinating and thoughts become confused. I am writing this book as a survivor, much like anyone suffering from any illnesses. My psychosis (hallucination) occurs because of a chemical imbalance between the serotonin and dopamine levels in my brain. Much serious concussion to the brain could be a possible factor too. It is also known that if one partner has the chemical imbalance, there is a fifty-fifty percent chance that the offspring may obtain mental health illness as well. In other words, it could be hereditary. When this happens, there are medications available to counteract the imbalance. It is similar to the way people with Type 1 Diabetes; they require insulin to balance their sugar level because their pancreas is not functioning well. Unfortunately, many view physical illness as acceptable, but not mental or emotional disorders. Yet many who suffer from Bipolar disorder or Manic Depression happen to be geniuses. Abraham Lincoln (a well-known president of the United States) is one of them; so are a few actors and actresses of the day, such as Jim Carrey and Catherine Zeta-Jones. I obtained this information from a televised program, Entertainment Tonight, about their lives.

Back to my state of psychosis at home: Mom started to install locks to keep me from leaving. However, I outsmarted her. I was still able to leave the premises, as the locks were not installed properly.

This time, I wore a cloak. I was trying to match my body image to that of Jesus; I thought he had a cloak with him two thousand years ago when his enemies put it on him. One day, I took the bus to a shopping mall. I can quite literally recall my own actions. I closed my eyes and gazed up toward the sun and spread out my hands on both sides, just like Jesus did on the cross. I heard some cars honking at me at the parking lot. I chose to ignore them.

Later on that day, I went into a building of condominiums that I had always desired to live in. I found myself in a stairwell. I thought the other side of the door was heaven. I kept knocking for God to let me in. With no response, I went up and down the stairs, chanted with some rituals in my mind, and did certain actions on my body to "get rid" of evil spells. I knocked even louder and more desperately. One lady opened the door after hearing me pounding on the other side. I quickly picked up my bag and found my way to the elevator, which a group of people were in. They started laughing, as I smelled of ammonia. Soon, the concierge was called in.

One of the concierges started to open up my belongings that I was carrying with me. He found my brother's phone number and address. I did not realize that they had called the police on me. The officers came with my brother and mom in their cruiser. I was taken in. Mom tried to console me, as I was frightened, not knowing that I was very ill. The police brought us home. The next day, at home, close to the window in my living room, I "saw" a shadow that I thought was my spirit leaving my body and flying up to heaven. I was naked, and Mom could not take it anymore. She called the police herself. Two officers came and took me to the hospital, to the psychiatric ward.

At the intake room, I was joking with the police officers—a man and a woman. I thought they were a couple I had known some time before. I did not know why I had been brought to the hospital. Suddenly, I woke up and saw what looked like a female giant monster sleeping next to me on another bed. I was strapped to my bed. I did not realize that, the night before, the doctor had authorized the nurse to inject me with some medication. When I woke up, I thought I was in heaven with a strange person next to me.

I did not realize that I was going to be hospitalized in the psychiatric ward for two solid months. Tom, one of my ex-boyfriends, would visit me almost every day, trying to encourage me to get well. I would be so frustrated when he said that I should calm down; I had no idea what he meant. I felt like I was in jail, with no freedom to get out of the hospital. When I was in a manic state, my energy level was high. However, my speech was not comprehensible. There were a lot of racing thoughts, and my thinking was all over the place. Before I could finish one subject, I would go on to the next. I would cut people off in mid sentence. This is the manic phase; these are my symptoms that I recognize in myself. Note that everyone has different degrees of hallucination. Some may have none, as they can think of ways to keep such a crisis from happening. It is all about educating yourself about mental health issues—(Bipolar, Depression, Panic Attacks, Schizophrenia, Obsessive-Compulsive Disorder, Epilepsy, any neurological disorder related to the brain cells.)

I was prescribed five different types of medication. They were very sedating. I felt that everything I did was very slow. The impact of it at that time was too painful for me to bear in the hospital. I would ask, "When can I get out?" It was too long a stay for me. How could I prove to the doctor and nurses that I was ready to go home? I had no knowledge of the illness; neither did I know any coping strategies at that time. It was mental torment for me each day as I stayed longer. I could neither write, nor read, nor sing, nor play the piano, nor remember. Neither could I speak fluently—complete mental agony for me. It was just as hard for my close ones to see me having such difficulty.

No one understood what I was going through. I questioned my own mentality. Was my thinking accurate, or was I crazy? It was a constant struggle for me. What would others think of me now? Would I be faced with this type of illness in the future? My hospital stay seemed so long. I lost my job during this time, and I was worried about how long it would take for me to recover fully. Financially, I was tight. I almost had to sell my car. While I was sick in the hospital, I incurred a huge debt, and in the end I had to go through credit counselling and pay up by instalments. My credit rating went from excellent to poor.

Eventually, I was allowed to leave the hospital on the weekends. The first time I went out of the hospital with Michelle, Tom's mother, and Tom himself, I was overwhelmed by the sight of everything around me. The shops seemed confusing to me. I was so addled from all the medication inside of me. I stayed overnight with them and was sad to return to the ward.

Being manic, I was also flirting with a man in the hospital. He fell for me and was heartbroken that he had to leave me there when he was discharged. He started contacting me, but I did not understand him, as he spoke French. Hence, the relationship was short-lived. My brief encounter with him was kept a secret for many years. I did not want Tom to be upset. At that time, I was not sure if the Frenchman was right for me. Flirting is a part of mania; many will not understand that this is one of the symptoms.

My relatives and friends would visit me at the hospital once in a while. At around this time, mom was a permanent resident; she came back to Canada to retain her status. Her visits were less frequent, as we did not get along at that time. I felt very hurt when the nurse told me that Mom did not want me to reside with her at home. She wanted me to be in a group home. However, at that time, I had not been a Canadian citizen for ten years, and so I was not eligible for financial help from the government. My parents could not afford to pay for my stay in the group home. So I returned to my own residence with Mom. She was afraid of my rages and would try not to anger me. I, on the other hand, was too tired to fight in any way. The medication made me sleep a lot, as I did not sleep very much when I was ill.

I started eating quite a bit; I put on a lot of weight, much to my dismay. Something about the new combination of medication made it impossible to contain my sweet tooth.

Most of the pills I took initially caused dry mouth, blurred vision (this disappeared as my body adjusted itself after a while), constipation, lack of concentration, lack of memory, and sedation. I requested a printout from the pharmacist to analyse these side effects, so that I could explain to the doctor how severe the side effects were. The doctor could either adjust the dosage or change to another type of medication that had fewer side effects. It was of the utmost importance to be open with the doctor in order to find the right combination of medications.

A couple of weeks later, I was told to attend a day treatment program at a hospital. It was a three-month program geared to helping patients return to a somewhat normal lifestyle, teaching basic coping strategies. I wrote as many notes as I could to benefit myself. I am proud to be a Canadian, as I believe that nowhere in the world could we find a program, assisted by the government, to help patients back to recovery. In Canada back then, mental and emotional disorders did not have as much stigma as they did in most other countries. At least in Canada, consumer survivors like us were allowed to return to work like everyone else.

After the program, I signed up for yet another twenty-week program at a college for rehabilitation, from which I obtained a certificate of completion. Thereafter, I started to look for a permanent job. I was employed in 1996. I worked for a year, and during my vacation, I decided to embark on a ten-day trip to the Mediterranean. I was elated when I reached England. From there, I flew to Spain, where I boarded a cruise ship. I had a great time on the cruise, which brought me to Southern France and Italy and back to Spain. However, when I arrived home to Canada, I started feeling depressed again. It seemed to me that travelling abroad triggered it. I read an article which indicated that people with Bipolar disorder were at risk of a manic phase when travelling east and a depressive phase when travelling west, because of the change in sleeping patterns. Soon, I had to resign from my job, but it was on good terms. I needed to rest again.

I am what the doctor classifies as a *rapid cycler*. This means that my mood swings fluctuate, with ups and downs more than four times a year. I was suicidal in 1997, depressed in 2004 and 2007. I learnt that it is essential to manage the highs so that the lows will not be extremely severe. It is all about pacing yourself. When you are feeling hyper and full of energy, you have to do things that will slow you down. Meditation (a relaxation and breathing technique) is one of them. This technique can be done in many ways and forms. On the other hand, if you are depressed, you have to force yourself to do things that will uplift you. Hobbies, for example, are a good way to boost your mood.

CHAPTER 3

Relapse

I was able to control my mania for fourteen years; unfortunately, I became manic again from March 2008 to March 2009. For the longest while, I wondered what the cause of it was. I was vigilant in taking all my medication. As I reflect on it now, I feel very strongly that it was the stress of my work that triggered the manic phase, as my work required a lot of multitasking. Stress was the trigger point of my illness, as it is for many others.

During my days of psychosis, Michelle knew I was very ill. Not that I was hurting anyone else, but I was personally going through many aches and pains all over my body. As I have come to realize, I was suffering from what psychiatrists would call the *tactile experience*, feeling "things" that are not there. I mentioned to Michelle that I consistently felt pain as I passed the electrical units in my bedroom. She decided to play along, not quite knowing what to do with me. One day when she came to visit, we decided to move my bed from the bedroom to the dining room to keep it from touching any electrical units. For a short period, I could sleep in the dining room without any aches and pain.

I called my brother Michael, to come for a visit, and suddenly I became suspicious of him, accusing him of siding with people who did witchcraft on me. I felt that he purposely came to visit me at the new condo that I'd bought for myself. I took note of the fact that he saw where my bed was placed. In my own mind, I believed that Michael and his gang were all out to get me, to hurt me by practising voodoo. The noise from my neighbour's upstairs sounded like a pipe creating droplets of water above me, constantly triggering pain in my head. Every night, my legs would be in pain, as I noticed the bed that was placed outside the dining area also had electrical units. I found that out later. I just had to bear with the pain.

One of the prominent thoughts I had, during the mania, was about my faith. I had converted from being a Baptist back to being a Catholic again. I started going to a Catholic church nearby. Mom was with me during the time I was sick, from March 2008 to November 2008. She had no idea that I was very ill. She was very happy regarding my conversion. One day, she gave me an advertisement for a Catholic store. I decided to go with Michelle to get some supplies there. We bought medals, crosses, and Fatima water. According to the store clerk, Fatima water came about when Mary, the mother of Jesus, appeared to three children in Portugal. Soon, as I was using the Fatima water, I began to "witness" miracles happening around me: that is, I thought that I was healing others of any illnesses, just like Jesus did in His days. Little did I know that I was seeing things that were not there.

Around the same month, I felt a painful twisted stab in my stomach. My mind suddenly imagined a huge pest above me; it had the shape of a sow bug. Physically, I felt that my whole body was sucked up by it. My thoughts were way off, misconstrued ideas hovering between reality, dreams, and nightmares. I started asking Michelle and Mary, my counsellor, for help with regards to the pain "caused" by people who did witchcraft on me. Of course, these ideas were part of my illness. I had two prayer letters to "counteract" the witchcraft.

My pain was very severe—so much so that I had to use mental rituals to block the pain. I had to deflect all my pain back to Jesus, as I thought that only He could take my pain. I had to say, in my mind, that my blood was Jesus's blood, which was a poison to people who performed witchcraft on me. My thinking was haywire, as nothing made sense to people around me.

I was seeing things through the television as well—thinking that the television was talking and telling me what to do, what to buy and where to move. It seemed to me that everyone who appeared on the television could see me at home, too. They all knew I was suffering a lot from all the witchcraft that was being done on me. Before long, a doctor who happened to be a bachelor, Dr. Paul Dwain, appeared on the television and, I thought, communicated with me by telepathy. Not long after, I stitched together a romantic connection between Paul and I in my mind. Faithfully every Monday to Friday from three to four p.m., I would turn on the channel to watch the doctors and "communicate" with Paul. I thought everyone in Hollywood and the Canadian government knew about me because of Paul's celebrity status. I even thought the Queen of England was watching me through my own television. My thoughts began to tell me that I had to dress up and behave well when she was watching me from home.

My mind drifted off to thinking that I had to get up to be on alert for any bad spirits coming into my abode. My sleeping patterns became absurd. I would sleep three hours some nights, other nights two hours, and once, I didn't sleep at all. During the times when I was awake, I would erratically watch the television or turn on the radio so that I would be informed of my next idea. I thought the television was predicting news or events about the world for me. Next, I began to feel very frustrated when things started "disappearing" on me. Michelle tried to find ways to tackle the problem. She invited a friend over. Her friend pointed out that an old way of dealing with witchcraft was to put a pair of scissors below the Bible. From that idea, instead of putting the scissors below my Bibles, I placed the scissors on top of all my Bibles. Every night, I would faithfully place a Bible with the scissors next to my pillow where my head was, thinking that it would protect me from voodoos done on me.

At one point, I installed an alarm system. Nearly every day or night, the system would trigger a loud sound. A security guard and a couple of police officers would arrive to see if there was a serious problem. At first, when the security guard arrived, I started to touch him from head to toe, saying the verse, "In His strive, that is, through Jesus's sufferings, you are healed." He did not think much about it—in fact, he thanked me for it. The verse came about as I was watching a Christian program. When the pastor said that, I started shortening the verse, "In His strive, that is, through Jesus' sufferings, you are healed," to the symbol O in my mind. This became my way of "chanting" in my prayers. Soon, I began equating all the chants with the symbol O to get rid of the pain in my body.

Then came the worse nightmare for me. I started sponsoring four children as I watched a Christian program: one each from Cambodia, Haiti, Zambia, and India. I went on to spend close to two thousand dollars on different charities that were asking for donations through the television. For many of them, I would use my credit cards, with donations deducted monthly. Next, I got a phone call from someone in America asking if I would like to buy some gold and silver coins. I started to max out all my credit cards just purchasing the coins. Little did I realize that I had spent CAN$60,000! I thought my imaginary boyfriend, Paul, and I would buy the coins to help with the world's bad economy. My logic was not quite there. I did not know how to help, but just to continue buying the coins. I thought that Paul would let me know the process of helping others when we could meet up in Los Angeles. In the back of my mind, I thought that China would soon be demanding gold and silver. When they continued to do so, we would sell the coins at a huge profit and start distributing the money to save the world.

The thoughts about witchcraft were what psychiatrists would term *conspiracy theories* (Beck et al. 1979). This, in simple words, means that I felt everyone was out to get me, and everyone blamed me for everything. I strongly felt that everyone blamed me for all the bad weather, accidents, and fires in buildings that occurred in Canada, and for the world's bad economy. My constant belief was that people wanted me dead because of what I did. The pain became so bad that Michelle invited me to sleep over at her place. I still hallucinated. I remembered clearly one night how I could not breathe at all; my mind was all over the place thinking that the people upstairs were doing witchcraft on me in Michelle's apartment. I had to get up and sit at an angle in order to breath and sleep.

I would literally see cars following me as I drove back and forth from my place to Michelle's. I would take zigzag routes or travel the longest way from one place to another. I took this to mean that the people were following me, that they were telling each other when and where I was going. Similarly, helicopters would fly above my home, and I thought they were tracing my whereabouts. Little did I know that it was a lack of sleep for several nights in a row that was causing my hallucinations. Strangely enough, at one point, I forgot about the witchcraft and started to think that Paul wanted me to practise being a mother by getting up at different times of the night.

One night, I filled a wine-bottle holder with all of the medals, the Cross of Jesus, and the bottle of Fatima water, and I placed it outside of my neighbours' condo two floors up. I kept thinking that they were my enemies. Later, I completely forgot that I was the one placing the objects there. I complained to Michelle that they were all stolen. My memory started to fade. I started to use the "blessed" salt and sprayed it under my bed to ward off bad spirits. The idea of the blessed salt came about as a man was selling Catholic items at a store; he mentioned to me about spraying the salt that is blessed by the priest, under my bed to ward off evil spirits.

I practised burning bottled candles at sunset for a couple of hours. One red thick candle had the face of Jesus; the other was a light green thick candle given to me as a gift. The red candle represented the blood of Christ, and the green one represented peace and hope. Each of the candles was dipped with a drop of the Fatima water using a cotton bud. I thought this daily ritual would injure the bad people practising witchcraft on me. Causing them pain was my constant idea of revenge. I thought that they should feel all the pain that they had inflicted on me. I would seal off the bottled candles with lids and water, thinking that my actions would stifle them.

In addition, I bought a scented oil brand that was advertised on television. It became a habit: whatever was advertised would be whatever I should buy. I started buying many things that were on TV. At one point, a Nissan commercial showed a voodoo doll being pricked at the back. The image seemed to confirm to me that voodoo was done on me. Whatever the storylines were on television, I was reading into them. One of the movies had a sci-fi theme dealing with witches. It ended with one of the actresses killing herself. I took the storyline and mentioned to Michelle that I had to kill myself in order to stop the people from hurting me further. Michelle was very upset when I mentioned it to her. She was very worried, to the point that she requested the help of a pastor. However, the pastor could not help me in my situation. Fortunately, the idea of killing myself was postponed . . . somehow, sometime, I forgot about it.

I started writing everything in red. The idea behind the red ink was that the devil would not be able to read whatever I wrote on paper, as it represented the blood of Christ. I thought that I was fortunate to have many pens with red ink. I thought that it was God's will for me to do so in order to tangle with the devil! I mentioned this to as many people as possible. I even sent Christmas cards all written in red.

I began to feel more pain during that time of the month, or during the times when I brushed my teeth with a little blood flowing into the sink. I began to hate it every time when I bled down the sink or the bathtub; the blood flowing down brought more pain in my body. At the blood lab I went to, I thought the nurse was scheming against me, using my blood. My knees would start jerking, and I thought the doctors not only hurt me by using my blood, they were also causing my knees to jerk. Another physical feeling was that I thought someone must be trying to make me fat, as I experienced bubbling sensations in my legs. I thought that my enemies were jealous of me for looking slim. By this time, I had lost a lot of weight—forty pounds in two months! I started attributing my weight loss to a health supplement that was advertised. Thinking back, it was horrific. I recalled there were times when I would lick sauces for lunch and dinner and ate minimally.

I mentioned earlier in this chapter being bothered by the noise of the elevator outside my condo. This noise became my way of communicating with my so-called enemies. For some strange reason, I used the Chinese form of thinking regarding the yin and the yang, the balance between water, air, fire, wood, and another element not present: metal. As the contractors were using equipment to drill holes outside, I felt the pain on my back. Each time they drilled, it felt like a hole was drilled in my back. In my head, I had to say, "Balance it using wood, fire, and water." This was short-formed to *O*, meaning, "In Jesus' suffering, we are all healed." I would touch my back, say the ritual, and the pain would be gone. Throughout that winter, in the middle of the night, as the snow was ploughed outside, I would feel pain in different parts of my body. Similarly, I had to press against each part and say "*O*," and the pain would disappear.

Sometime during 2008, I brought my car to a dealership for a free installation of some sort. Wires were hooked to the back of my trunk. About a month after the installation, I started having a strong suspicion that my car had been implanted with a microphone that I could not locate. As I turned on the engine of my car, talking in my car became another form of ritual, time and time again. I thought everyone out there could hear me through this microphone. At one point, I announced that whoever bought my home, he or she would prosper and be blessed, as my residence has two lucky number 7s on my door. Why did I announce that in my car, "through the microphone" that I thought was installed by my dealership? Well, I wanted to sell my condo a few months after buying it. Paul, the doctor in the States, I thought, wanted me to be with him in California, away from the people who were practising voodoo on me. The height of my mania came when I decided to fly to Los Angeles, California, with a one-way ticket via Calgary. I thought that Paul would be meeting me there. I hallucinated throughout the flight, from my stopover in Calgary until I arrived at the airport in Los Angeles.

CHAPTER 4

Hospitalization

When we landed in the Calgary airport, a voice told me (I was hearing voices that were not there, telling me what to do) that I had to move away from the plane as quickly as I could. I thought to myself, *I'm glad the plane entrance is just a door ahead of me.* I quickly took my small baggage and left the plane in a hurry. I felt that I had to run for my life, as the plane was going to explode and the fire could catch up with me. This, again, was all in my mind. I reached the counter and asked for my luggage. I became suspicious when the representative told me to get it at the wrong area. I finally found my luggage after I overheard her telling another passenger the right place. I went up to her again, asking where I could get the shuttle bus that was supposed to be there to pick me up. Again she gave me the wrong directions. I took a dislike toward her and branded her as part of the gang.

I had to wait for a few minutes before the shuttle van picked me up. I reached my hotel, but I did not sleep much, as I felt that I had to stay alert regarding any witchcraft. I showered in the dark, with very little light on. I covered myself to sleep with a winter coat. It seemed like only a couple of hours before I woke up. I was rather anxious that I would miss my plane to Los Angeles. I chided the receptionist for not calling me.

It was Christmas Day when I arrived at the LA airport and started searching for Paul. There was no sign of him at all! I waited next to a security guard until late in the evening. The guard was actually watching me, as he knew that I was very sick. I grew tired of waiting, and I started to ask the next guard for help. He said that he could not help me with the witchcrafters who were ganging up against me. As I walked along the pathway, my feet were hurting, so I took my shoes off. Very shortly, I saw a police station. I ran toward it and told a female police officer that I needed to be in custody. A group of people went up to her and mentioned something. Immediately, another police officer handcuffed me and brought me to UCLA Medical Center. There, I was forced to stay at the psychiatric ward for ten days, from December 25, 2008, to January 5, 2009.

My short stay was surprisingly pleasant for me. I made friends with some of the nurses and the patients. The nurses kept telling me not to talk about witchcraft; otherwise I would have difficulty leaving. I told them that Paul knew me and that I was to marry him. Time and time again, I tried to get his phone number, but to no avail. I also mentioned to the nurses about the Fatima water, how it protected me. I was talking about my faith constantly. Although the hospital's temperature was low, the food was excellent. On January 5, I was sad to leave the hospital, as the staff treated me well. They even cooked a meal ahead of time before I boarded the plane with my uncle back to Toronto. They did not even charge me any amount during my stay in the hospital.

Back in my home again, I was shocked that my car was still at the airport, when I had specifically written a note for it to be picked up. This note was written and left in my home. Of course, no one would know. I was too sick to understand. Worst of all, someone had damaged the back of my car. I concluded that it was the gang again. When I reached home, I kept in contact with Mary and my Aunt Celina. I kept asking them for prayers, as my pain was back. I started to hallucinate again, thinking that the UCLA doctors and nurses were defending me from afar, helping me to stop those who were supposedly practising witchcraft on me. Round and round again, I had to go through the rituals in my mind.

On January 21, I was supposed to have an appointment with a new psychiatrist, but he would not accept me as a patient. Mary, my counsellor, felt that I should be hospitalized but was fearful that I would not cooperate. We went to a restaurant and had lunch. I gorged down all I could, as I had not been eating much for days. I was quite anorexic. This is common when one is in the manic phase. Mary tricked me by saying that if I went into the hospital, I would be able to help a lot of people there. She said that it was hard to find counsellors in the hospital, and that I could pretend to be a counsellor during my stay. In this way, she enticed me to be admitted to the hospital. We went to the hospital and waited there for hours. Later, my aunt came to wait with me and relieve Mary of her duties.

My hospital stay was much the same. Wherever I walked, I had constant physical aches and pains in my head and body. My body would be afflicted with a sharp pain on my feet. I had to use rituals in my head every time I used the washroom and when I walked out from my room to the hallway. This way, the pain would miraculously disappear. Time and time again, I told the doctor that Paul was my fiancé . . . until I found out that he was dating someone else secretly. I happened to read it in a magazine. I was devastated. However, I had many visitors during my stay in the hospital; therefore, I was able to seek comfort from them. When it came to my brother's visit, I would tell him off constantly, thinking that he was involved in a gang. I began demanding that my brother and his gang pay off all my credit card bills.

On February 24, 2009, my psychiatrist allowed me to stay overnight at my own home. I had to pull off the cushions from the sofa bed and sleep on the floor—again, avoiding the electrical units. I went back to the hospital the next morning and mentioned to the doctor that I slept well, though I lied and said that I slept in my own bed. At this time, he was not aware that I had physical pains as well. Based on what I said to him, he decided to discharge me from the hospital, much to Mary's dismay. She knew that I was not ready at all. She refused to take me home. However, I managed to get a hold of my aunt. She had to drive all the way back to the hospital in the evening to bring me home.

When I arrived home, I was still hallucinating for the whole month of March, 2009. I managed to get an appointment with my own psychiatrist outside of the hospital. Through the intelligence of another doctor, he tried me on a different set of medication: Epival, Seroquel, and Clonazapam. Very soon, my hallucinations stopped. My doctor recommended a Day Clinic program for me as an outpatient, which is associated with the hospital. To many, my recovery seemed amazingly fast as I sought help from the program. It was hard work going through the program each day. It was all about acceptance of the relapse, changing from negative to positive thinking, self-empowerment, embracing the "live for the present day" concept, stress management, anxiety, and symptom management with relaxation techniques. Exercise was of utmost importance as well. Not only did it curb the weight gain from the medication, it helped alleviate depression. Relaxation could involve light yoga exercises, deep breathing, or imagining oneself in the middle of a beautiful setting with relaxing music in the background. There are many forms, such as tai chi and chi gong. All can help you to slow the pace and slow yourself down. They are about achieving the ultimate balance in your life, and in your mental and physical health.

CHAPTER 5

Recovery

Bipolar disorder, or Manic Depression, is an illness that affects thoughts, feelings, perceptions and behaviour—even how a person feels physically. It is not about, "Oh, it's all in your mind." There is strong evidence that the disorder is caused by a chemical imbalance in the brain. Before I discuss my personal coping strategies, I would like to emphasize the importance of group therapy.

When I was discharged from the hospital, I attended a Day Clinic program for mental health outpatients. I realize that not all the provinces in Canada, and not all other countries, have such a program. I would highly suggest that those other provinces of Canada and countries send doctors, counsellors, and therapists to attend, study, and analyze for themselves the effectiveness of Day Clinic programs for clients. Through these programs, many have returned to full-time or part-time work; or back to studying in schools or universities again.

I'll give you a quick idea of how the Day Clinic works. One is assigned to a case coordinator who works with the client to monitor progress, set goals, offer support and resources, reassess issues discussed in the group, and at the final stage, make discharge plans. In order for clients to benefit from the program, it is very important that they participate in as many programs as possible with an honest, open-minded attitude and strong willpower to relearn new skills in order to survive their chronic illness.

Acceptance of illness is an important head start to recovery. Once a client accepts the illness, the patient has already reached the 50 percent level of recuperation. Next, cooperation with the doctors, therapists, and nurses is vital. Taking medication, for example, is crucial. From my personal experience, I know that I must monitor my medication side effects alongside my doctor. Know your medication well. Read the labels carefully as to when you need to take them—either in the morning, evening, or night—and understand what each medication is for. Find out if it can be mixed with other medications or even health supplements. Quite a number of medications specify that the use of alcohol may increase sedation. Therefore, abstain from the use of alcohol.

When any new medication is prescribed to me, I ask for a printout from the pharmacist in order to study the side effects of the medication on my body. The initial side effects for me are an inability to sit down to do a task or stand up for a long period of time, and an urge to walk in circles or back and forth—both symptoms of restlessness. I inform my doctor about it, and he will either adjust the dosage or put me on another pill that will control my restlessness. Clients have to learn how to communicate openly with their doctors about the side effects of medications and any stressful situations they may be facing. There are many possible side effects, including blurred vision, dry mouth, tremors in the hands or legs, and weight gain. However, this does not mean that whenever one has, for example, blurred vision or dry mouth, it will be there all the time. At this point, the doctor may still not stop the medication. The psychiatrist may adjust the dosage, and eventually the symptoms will cease to exist. For some, it may take a month to several months before the side effects dissipate. It is also vital to go for blood tests once or twice a year to make sure that the medication's effects will not be overly potent.

One tip that I find very useful for myself is to chart my mood, irritability, sleep, concentration, energy, and motivation in my diary daily. I rank them all from one to ten. One indicates my lowest level, eight is my steady level, and anything above eight signifies hypermania. I also write down my perception of things around me: what is upsetting me for the day or any stressors in my life. Since the doctor does not know how I function on a daily basis—as he only sees me once a week or once a month—the chart in my diary will indicate to him how I feel regularly. This way, there is no guessing game between us. Ultimately, the doctor will find the right combination of medication. A particular combination may work for one person but not for others. One combination of pills does not fit all. Finding the right combination of medication for a particular individual patient requires trial and error.

Some doctors do both prescription and counselling, while others do prescription only. This is where the Day Clinic comes into play. I would highly recommend that individuals sign up with a psychotherapist, case worker, or social worker in their local area if they do not have such facilities. Now that most people have access to a computer, they can easily find out which hospitals offer Day Treatment programs. Search under mental and emotional disorders, and treatments for them.

The treatment offered in the Day Clinic works around the concept of Cognitive Behavioural Therapy, as described in the book *Cognitive Therapy of Depression* (Dr. Ronald Fieve: Moodswings, 1989, Pg. 176). Honesty and willingness to relearn positive thinking skills during group discussions are fundamental. The therapists or nurses who lead each class have a clear understanding of the various stages of regression or improvement in their clients. Patients who choose not to speak openly about issues that are bothering them are the ones who will not benefit from Day Treatment. This is just my personal opinion. One needs to attend as many classes offered by the Day Clinic as possible; three times a week is the minimum recommendation. In each of the classes, patients are encouraged to participate and work on their issues. This way, the therapists, nurses, and doctors in the program will be able to access each patient, as they hold meetings twice a week.

I will give you a highlight of what the day-treatment classes offer:

- group therapy
- stress management
- symptom management
- crisis prevention
- help with self esteem
- anxiety management
- anger management
- mind-over-mood instruction
- personal development
- assertiveness training
- help for family and life issues
- instruction in weight management, low-sugar living, and wellness
- physical exercises/light yoga classes
- instruction on relationship techniques
- art therapy
- positive psychology
- motivational-metaphor group
- activity group
- brain-fitness training
- friendship circle

- groups for music appreciation, current events, weekly movies, humour, and inspiration

An elaboration on the classes and what I have learnt from each will be offered in the following chapters. As for me, from each counsellor and the friends I selected on my own, I have learnt to pick and choose the best ideas that will work out for me, to improve myself and stay strong from within.

CHAPTER 6

Recognizing Signs and Symptoms

The initial step toward symptom management is all about awareness and understanding of yourself. What you can do for yourself is read about the signs and symptoms of your illness, after the diagnosis. Read as many self-help books as you can that include not only the signs and symptoms, but also important coping strategies. If you are not sure which books to read, ask your doctor or therapists or case workers. They will gladly recommend books to you. The other option is to find book recommendations on legitimate websites, which I have mentioned under my references.

By attending the day clinic and reading as much as possible, I found out what my own signs and symptoms are and watch out for them when I am about to get ill again. This is called *crisis prevention*. From a Manic Depressive point of view, I have gone through the stable mood swings, Mixed state, Hypomania, Mania, and Depressive phases. When I am in the phase of mania, I giggle, and my speech becomes erratic and loud. All my hearing senses are heightened: I hear everything very loudly, too. I will become extremely angry, almost uncontrollable, over issues that are not of any importance. At this point, I will spend a lot, see things on the television and hear things that are not there, and hardly sleep at all. I begin to lose a lot of weight as well at this point in time. My speech becomes very rapid, and I will not listen to others' conversation—many times, I will not allow them to even finish their sentences. It is very difficult to control, as my mind at that point is racing.

In Chapter 2, I mentioned that I am what psychiatrists call a *rapid cycler*. This means that my mood swings occur more than four times a year, even though I take my medication regularly. Though I am writing about my own illness, the steps toward healing are similar with other mental health issues. One of the signs of depression is a sad mood filled with anxiety and worry. Sleep is affected; there are appetite changes and weight changes. One becomes very lethargic, with little energy to do even simple tasks like bathing and cooking. In severe cases, suspicion or paranoia is quite common. One's perspective changes, and the individual may become extremely pessimistic as negative thoughts arise. Things get blown out of proportion. Eventually, it becomes very difficult for the individual to make decisions. Concentration and memory will be affected; eventually, confusion will take over. Irritability arises—some patients show extreme anger and/or violence that is almost incontrollable. One becomes upset easily and is very sensitive to situations and other people. It is quite common for sensitivity to occur in patients who have mental health issues.

As for hypomania, this is the stage where it is before the manic phase strikes. Bear in mind that everyone has different symptoms;

individuals will need to identify for themselves what their signs are. The manic stage is where the crisis has already occurred where hallucination and paranoia are common. My general symptoms are lack of sleep; decreased appetite followed by loss of weight; being easily angered, with racing thoughts; increased level of energy; giggling and laughing at things that may not be funny; and being very talkative, with my voice level becoming louder as well. My senses become heightened with the ability to hear things very clearly from far off, and there is a sudden alertness to the environment around me. Creativity is best at this level. I become very artistic and vibrant, with a strong desire to wear colourful clothing. Restlessness also sets in. Flirtatiousness is not uncommon. Spending becomes an issue; it is very difficult to stop buying unnecessary things. In my worst-case scenario, I had contributed over four thousand dollars to charity organizations and sponsored four children from different parts of the world.

At work, I would be able to multitask at such a speed that almost no one in the work environment could keep up with me. Many times, unknowingly, it became a problem, as some colleagues would be jealous of me; they thought I was making them look bad since they could not do as much as I could. I would stand out and become a favourite of my employers, much to the dismay of some of my colleagues. Then the cycle would begin. Some colleagues would start creating problems for me, for example, gossiping or trying to find my weak spots. The bottom line was, I was dealing with many people with insecurities within themselves. They wanted to put me down so that their own self-esteem would be raised. Hence, there was bullying against me. Wherever I worked, I faced the same negative situation. However, I did have a few colleagues I enjoyed working with; some treated me with respect, and others were amazed at how I could accomplish many tasks all at once. Back to the problem in dealing with people who are insecure and have a tendency to bully one another, there is a positive solution to this. It starts with being assertive. Mind you, it is not about being aggressive. This is one of the ways you can prevent yourself from being extremely hurt and, thereafter, stressed.

CHAPTER 7

Coping Strategies Using the Positive Power of the Mind

In this chapter, I will share with you some strategies I have learnt for remaining positive and staying in control of my mental health. Not all of them may work for you, but you may find something here that will help you. It seems that problems surface with stress that leads to many health issues; hence, strategies are important before the crisis begins. I will give you a synopsis of what I have learnt from my past experience: increase one's self-esteem by being assertive; discovering your hobbies; focusing on self care; being selective in cultivating friendships; finding a support group; no blame games and negative thoughts; anger management; maintaining self control; realising that laughter is the best medicine; appreciating silence and putting an end to worrying; pacing oneself; improve memories through organization; managing weight gain; get enough rest; maintaining a good financial budget; staying on medication; being thankful and having faith. The details are as mentioned below:

Being Assertive

Assertiveness is all about excellent communication skills, with diplomacy in getting your ideas across to others and asking others their true opinion of how the work must be done. Most of all, observe the culture of the company. Some companies are laid back, then go with the flow. Do not stand out so much that others get jealous of you; keep everything low-key. However, if the company is based on a multitasking culture, be very careful you don't stress yourself out. Especially when one has mania, one uses all the energy on all types of various projects and ends up getting sick, and some even experience blackout. Watch out for yourself; know your limits and work within them.

Tackle the problem of gossips which leads to misunderstandings. You must be assertive and state to others that you are not interested in hearing gossip; this will keep the situation from getting worse. You have to stand up for what you truly believe and not be overly defensive. Before I attended the assertiveness classes at the clinic, I was not at all assertive—and worse, I was very sensitive to people's criticisms. I would keep quiet about what actually bothered me at work, only to explode at a later stage. This was not my colleagues' or my employers' problem—it was mine. I allowed it to happen. If I had learnt to be assertive, state in a precise way how I wanted to be treated, and stand up for myself, this would not have occurred. The problem with many of us is that we tend to blame others, but we do not take responsibility for how we react to a problem. One common phrase is: 10 percent is the problem, 90 percent is how you react. Would you allow bullying, for example, to consume you with anger? Of course, the answer is no! If you are upset by negative situations caused by toxic people, that can lead to lack of sleep. Just step away when you encounter a negative situation with someone. Avoid it. Otherwise, the pot of water inside of you will boil over, as the expression goes, causing anger and bitterness with others and yourself. Suddenly, you will find yourself unable to sleep, and that will lead to depression. Deep depression could very easily contribute to hallucinations.

Managing Stress by Discovering Your Hobbies

Because of my high sensitivity, when I become upset about a situation, I start doing things to distract myself from focusing on the problem when I reach home. Do not bring work home! That is, do not bring home problems caused by people who may have irritated you at work and then dwell on them at home. Your evenings are for you. Relax and enjoy yourself. One of the things that has helped me is finding out what my hobbies are. I enjoy painting, reading, playing the piano, solving puzzles, listening to music, exercise and watching television. What I am trying to emphasize here is that no matter how bad the situation you are faced with at work, you need to develop some hobbies. This way, you will not allow too much negative thinking that will eventually bog you down and further the cycle of depression.

Painting and sketching also became my therapy. My thoughts stop racing when I'm painting, and my energy level is focused on my drawings. Everyone has different ideas of how to enjoy life, so it is important for you to discover what your hobbies are. Identify the things that make you happy. Find out more about nature—the flowers in the fields, the sunlight, the moon, the starry skies, even the clouds. Explore your imagination. Go out and breathe in the fresh air. Trace the trails through parks and enjoy the forest, the sounds of the birds, and the cute sight of furry animals.

Do some self-care, no matter how difficult. Women, put on a little makeup, and you may feel special. Men, shave yourself clean, and perhaps you will feel better. Wash your hair and take a shower daily. Sometimes, when you are depressed, you need to push yourself to do these things. If you do not help yourself, not even God can help you, let alone your friends.

Another solution is to have a pet, if you can afford to one. It is therapeutic to have one; when you are sad, you can always pretend to talk to your pet. When you are able to look after your pet, your pet will learn to love you all the more.

Find your favourite sports and play with a friend or two—maybe ping pong, tennis, badminton, basketball or hockey. Have an open conversation with your friends. Reminiscing about the good times and laughing at yourself could pull you through the day. While socializing with positive individuals, you will learn to enhance each other's lives. Who knows, friends may have their own hobbies and invite you to, perhaps, learn a new instrument with them.

Learning new things will enlighten your mind. Perhaps your friends will encourage you to learn different crafts, like sewing, knitting, crocheting, baking, and jewellery-making; or learning how to play Sudoku, checkers or cards. All these are new tricks you could use to train your mind and divert yourself from delving so deep into your own roundabout negative thinking.

One of my favourite activities is hopping over to a friend's place to help with his garden. It is just a great feeling to pull all the weeds, put in new seedlings in the springtime, and watch the beautiful flowers and herbs grow right in front of me in the summertime. Enjoy the birds of the air flying around you. One day, I even had a friend who asked me out for a walk in my home surroundings, and we ended up studying the names of all the flowers and trees when we were walking by the park and the homes of others. I had such great admiration for this friend of mine who is a senior and is extremely knowledgeable about the names. When you start truly admiring your friends, how much they have blessed you, it brings forth good feelings.

There are abundant ways to use your talents to the full. One of the many things I like to do when I am restless, to slow me down, is to decorate my home by putting new pictures up on the wall, or hanging some wall sconces around to beautify my place. I look for good deals at different stores to find items at reasonable prices so I don't spend too much. While you're dressing up your home, you might also like to consider dressing yourself up. With all the dresses, blouses, skirts, shorts, and everything I have in the closet, I can mix and match when I have time to myself at home. Then I will not get bored and restless, and drive out to the stores and buy more new clothes. This is how I solve my high mood swings.

I always try to make sure that I keep myself clean. I pace myself; I wash my clothes on the weekend when the electrical costs are at their lowest. I make sure that I iron my clothes on a day when it is cool, so that I do not have to face the heat of the sun later on. There are many practical ways to do things to make yourself comfortable. Even when there are times I do not like ironing, I will remind myself that if I do not iron the clothes on a cool day, I will not feel comfortable when the temperature of my home reaches over 30 degrees Celsius. I try to look and feel good when I meet others outside of home, even when my mood is low.

Many times we have to force ourselves to do things so that we can make ourselves feel useful once again. I used to feel helpless and hopeless; I don't feel it very much now, knowing at the back of my mind that whatever I am feeling will soon be over. This is because I have come to terms with my illness. I have gained a lot more understanding of the nature of Manic Depression over the years. I realize that this illness can be controlled, though not 100 percent cured, by medication. However, half the battle is over, provided that I stick to my decision to take the pills for the rest of my life.

Focusing on Self-Care and Self-Awareness

Self-care can also come in the form of realizing that not everyone likes you. Everyone clashes. Conflicts are always present. The main thing is to get issues resolved so that the job is done. When you are depressed at work, tell yourself that despite the way you feel, you are still able to work. Say to yourself: "I am the unsung hero, not a victim." You need to do some self-monitoring to see if you are in touch with reality. Now, knowing full well that my mood swings are easily triggered by stress, and fearing recurring swings in the future, I have come to lower my self-expectation when it comes to my career. Instead of working at the management level, I have settled for administrative work, where there will be less stress.

I must constantly adjust my lifestyle. My memory at times has been impaired, so I write things down in an appointment book to remind myself of my schedule for the day or future dates. Time and time again, I question myself: is my thinking accurate, or is it based on suspicion? Sometimes, if it gets worse, it will lead to a paranoia stage where I may think that everyone hates me. There will always be challenges ahead of me in terms of this illness. I will have to control my highs so that I will not hit the lows for a long period of time. I will always have to monitor my mood swings, informing my doctor of all the signs and symptoms. One of the major milestones that triggered my decision to take medication for the rest of my life is the fact that I do not want to be admitted to the hospital again. Neither do I want to waste yet another year on disability.

Cultivating Friendships

Sometimes, when I am in a joyful state, I will pick up the phone, chat with friends, and find out how they are doing. It's not about you only; you would like to know their feelings and state of mind as well. When you give positive vibes that you really care for your friends, they will appreciate you all the more, as you are genuinely concerned about them. However, in this state I can often become a chatterbox. I have to honour other people's point of view, give them time to express their opinions, and respect differences—then all will end well for both parties. Do favours for one another; take care of your other friends, if it is within your means. This produces a sense of fruitfulness and satisfaction within yourself. It is extremely therapeutic when you know that you have found true friends around you when you choose to decide to put others first.

One of the things I find amusing is going on Facebook. Initially, I was really shy about going on it. However, it's exciting when you find classmates you haven't seen for almost thirty years. I accidentally found a friend from my hometown who had moved to Canada. She paid me a visit with her family, and it was an emotional day for me in a positive way. We enjoyed each other's company to the fullest. When you think of past friends, try very hard to only remember the good things they have done for you. After all, life is too short to moan over spilt milk. We never know—the life of a friend may be gone in a moment. I recollected when I fought with a friend, I had to lower my pride and apologize. I thought about what the other person might have felt, listening to my outburst. When it comes to friends, cherish them while you have them. If you have none, well, start making more friends. Go to the mall and sit around. Who knows, you may encounter someone similar to you who shares all the experiences you have had in your lifetime.

Part of the healing process that facilitated my recovery was trying not to see myself as a victim. I use my illness positively, reaching out to others—for example, to some of my own family members and friends in whom I have detected some form of mental issues. Letting them know the symptoms of the illness and the various coping strategies, just as I have been counselled, does not leave me much room for self-pity.

Reversing Negative Thoughts with a Support Group

Be mindful what type of companions you are with. Negative people make others negative. Be selective of the friends you have; choose people who will not put you down but will encourage you all the way. With these friends, you may practise reversing your negative thoughts, guilty feelings, and regrets by refocusing on all the pleasant thoughts of your past involvement with your childhood friends who are good to you, and achievements you have done in your lifetime with family members or good friends.

You need to force yourself to move out of your comfort zone to find more friends and support groups to belong to. These groups help us understand each other's perspectives, share our experiences, and pick out all the good points from each individual that we can learn from. The support group could be in a day treatment program in which there are group therapies. Within the support groups, there is a one-on-one program where the client is being assessed on his or her progress. This is an outpatient program that many hospitals provide; just check the website. If your country does not have a program like this, do not let it stop you. Find out more information from books—it could be e-books or textbooks that you can purchase. If you cannot afford to buy them, look for them at a library close to you.

Banning Blaming and Avoiding Negative Thoughts

We need to be determined in our efforts to get better and not subject ourselves to negative thinking. Negative thoughts can appear in many forms, including questions and statements like "why . . . why did I not . . . what if . . . I should . . . I should have . . . I must . . . yes, but." These words are detrimental to our progress. They are words of regret. Yes, you may take medication to help with your recovery, but the other part that requires a lot of work is learning to be more positive in your thinking. We need to have strong willpower to change our thoughts, as our mindset will affect our attitude, our behaviour, and finally our health. The choice to make a change for the positive is up to you. No one can force you. It's all about positive affirmation. Within yourself, you need a strong will to overcome yesterday's problems. Do not regress and focus on past bad events. You need to move forward in a positive way. Just live a day at a time. Today has enough problems of its own. Tell yourself, "It's okay to make mistakes, everyone does it." Just try not to repeat them. Looking back at a bad past history will not produce any good results for anyone, not even for you. It may actually result in a self-fulfilling prophecy! Do not blame yourself or anyone else; neither is going to solve any problems. Blaming will just worsen every situation. Don't put yourself down or engage in self-pity. Learn to pat yourself on the back for once. If you can't, no matter how much time you invest in therapy, the road to recovery will be much slower, with little improvement. You must want to change yourself in your thoughts, words, and actions. Let the negative past be past. Don't dwell on it—choose to develop within yourself a positive mindset. Turn around your weaknesses to become your strengths. After all, many who are successful failed many times before that success.

You have to believe in yourself, identify your strengths, and acknowledge your weaknesses. Upon accepting your weaknesses, you will try to find ways to better yourself. Do not say words like,

"Oh, I'm crazy," "I will never be able to recover," and "Why did I not see it coming?" Stop beating yourself up. You have to unlearn all the negative sentences in your mindset that you have accumulated over the years, so that you can de-stress yourself in negative situations. Again, this requires lots of determination and willpower. The bottom line is this: people respond to their own failures, regrets, guilty feelings, and constant complaints about their negative past. Blaming others or yourself will never resolve a negative situation. The most important thing is to remind yourself that this is just a temporary state. It is hard to wipe off and block off your past history within yourself. Simply say to yourself, "Whatever happened before will help me change for the better and become wiser when problems arise again." In other words, learn from your past mistakes, and do not repeat them again in the future. Let all your negative thinking of the past be thrown into the sea of forgetfulness. The danger of being reminded of your bad past will cause you to have a broken spirit.

You may even choose to look at failure as part of a learning process. Do not be self-judgmental. Instead of putting negative ideas in your mind, you need to say to yourself, "I think I can, I know I can get better." Eventually, you will. Perhaps another phrase with which you may encourage yourself is, "I'm learning something new today, especially on improving my self-esteem." It may take time. That's life, so what? When you have been negative all your life, it definitely requires a lot of effort, strong willpower, and time to improve your thinking. Your willingness to take action is what matters. Learn from your mistakes and go on to live one day at a time. It is all about setting your own boundaries and balancing your own life.

Managing Anger by Problem-Solving

One of the opposites of positivism is anger. I've realized that, throughout my life, the root cause of my anger has been insecurity within myself. I was angry within myself; I didn't know what I was good for. When I was young, I was never a good student, especially from grade one to grade five. One of my teachers would hit my hand with a ruler, throw my exercise book on the ground, twist my ear, and hurt my poor ego. I began to cultivate a broken spirit. After those incidents, I was constantly at the bottom of my class in terms of grades. One day, my dad decided to pick me up by lifting my spirits with encouragement. He started to teach me how to study properly. That year, I became the the "best progress" girl in the whole school. I became the joy of my family. It was then that I realized that I did have good potential, with a little tug of love from my family.

When I entered the workforce, new problems started to arise. I was so used to being defended by my true friends and family that I never learnt how to develop excellent communication skills. These aren't about how well you speak, but how well you get your point across to the other party who is feeling insecure and threatened because your work is better than theirs, or you're more productive than they are. Many times, I would be bullied by colleagues who would spread rumours about me, such as, "She might take my job away." It came to a point where people started ganging up on me, much to my disappointment. I kept the hurt and injury to myself until one day, I exploded at work. I had to take sick leave. Another time, men would sexually harass me, and I could not defend myself. I had no one to turn to but my family, but they were far away in the Far East. Fortunately, in my later years, I learnt to distance myself from people who simply love to gossip about people around them, including me. Just walk away from the situation!

I had to seek counselling from my case worker. I learnt many things about being assertive without being aggressive. It is all about making statements like, "I understand that you may be having a bad day today. Is there something I could do to help both of us clear out any negative feelings?" This way, your colleague will realize that you are genuinely concerned about him or her. You both can start talking things out in a civil way without a shouting match or foul language. Having an emotional disorder tends to make one overly sensitive; just don't take things in a personal way, or you may blow things up in your own mind.

Sometimes others may have a bad day and just dump it on you. Don't let them . . . just walk away. You can empathize, but that's about it. It's other people's problems. We cannot help them if they cannot help themselves. Don't keep second-guessing that the fault is with you. You cannot control someone else's moods. If they choose to misunderstand you even if you try to explain, it is their problem, not yours. You are not at work to please everyone and have a strong desire to get their approval. You have to work hard at looking within yourself for your own security, instead of seeking approval from others. Learn to trust yourself. This assurance can only come from within. I have to take care of myself before I can help others. Stay away from gossip or being the office clown. You will fall into the trap of spiralling down to your own demise.

If people really upset you, learn to let go of your anger by redirecting your thoughts and channelling them to reach a wellness level. This is done by distracting yourself and keeping yourself busy all the time when you are at home. If you cannot let go of the negative work situation, document everything that happened during the negative events: this is called "journaling". With proper documentation of how others treat you at your workplace, you will have evidence that others are truly harassing you. You can also bring this documentation to your doctor or your counsellor; this way, you can be helped in all directions. Another helpful tip is this: If I have negative suspicions of situations or people, I will challenge them by writing down the negative points in a journal. After a few days, I will analyze and see if I am within focus. This way, my anger will not escalate to an uncontrollable state. It may be difficult initially, but always say to yourself, "I can do it. I know I can and I will do it." That should take away all the anger that is inside of you.

Be flexible and adaptable to positive changes within yourself. You do not need to carry all that baggage inside of you. There is hope when you seek it. Persevere, and your character will be much stronger. In the end, it's all about perception. Take control of your own situation, and you will prosper from within. Self-awareness is of utmost importance to achieving success in your lifetime.

Maintaining Self-Control

This leads to the concept of self-control, which may be very difficult to achieve, as you read along. It is about respecting the other person's point of view despite differences and offering a listening ear without barging in with your own opinion first. The other person will be more open to your opinion and more open-minded to your ideas when you show respect. Self-control is all about "mind over matter" (Bartlett, 2002).

It seems as though we live in a dog-eat-dog world, where it is all about listening to me and me only. In fact, we need to have the willpower to be open-minded, learn from one another, and see who has a better idea about overcoming personal difficulties. Ask others their ways of improvement instead of moping over your own sorry state of mind. Try to think outside the box. In other words, think before you talk. From my own experience, I learnt to be open-minded; I learnt all types of ideas and opinions from others; I picked the best positive solution for every negative situation. I chose to be accountable for my own actions and take full responsibility for my behaviour, and not accuse anyone of causing bad situations that happened to me. I tried to see the best in others and encourage them to move forward and think positively too. It's not a matter of controlling people or telling others what to do. In the end, since we live in a free country, others will make their own choices and deal with their own consequences.

Self-control is also about "mind over mood" (Beck et al. 1979, 11). Your problems may not be as bad as you think, if only you would listen carefully to what the other individual has gone through in his or her life, and what has brought him or her to their point of despair. When you show true care, concern, and respect for others and extend your help to your colleagues or friends or even acquaintances, people will draw very close to you eventually. Of course, you are not in it for a popularity contest; no, it is not about that. It is about self-respect and respecting others as well.

Once problems are resolved, when you get home, just let them go and don't dwell on them anymore. If something bothers you so much, write it down, analyse it at home, and brainstorm solutions. Ask yourself, did you overreact? Was it due to a situation that was blown out of proportion? Is your thinking distorted? Did you perceive incorrectly what others merely made as a comment to you?

Analyse your own thinking, otherwise it will affect your mood. A problematic matter that is not resolved during the day will lead to a problematic mood cycle. This will eventually lead to more stress that you do not need at all. If you have realized that you were in the wrong, do not be proud and refuse to acknowledge it. Apologize to others when you have done wrong, or your guilt will gradually eat you up inside. With guilt, you become depressed, and thereafter, you lose sleep. With a lack of sleep, you become confused and agitated all the time. This cycle of spiralling down in your own mind will not improve. Ask for help if you have reached this point—from a doctor, psychotherapist, psychiatrist, or even a close friend.

Remember, though, when you talk to your friends, the conversation must not always be about you, or you may end up stressing them out. There is always a balance to everything. Even if you know that you are right, and still others are judgmental of you, it is not your problem. Most of the time, people who are jealous of you feel insecure within themselves. Try to put yourself in other people's situation, and accept yourself and others as much as you can. It is all about self-respect and respecting others' differences, be it their ideas, opinions, faith, or suggestions. Do not judge others; be quick to listen and slow to anger. This way, you will live a bountiful life. A practical way to indulge in relaxation is this: when you get home after a long day of work, relax, take a nice shower, read a magazine, watch a comedy, listen to soothing music, and find a hobby to do.

When you realize that you have made wrong decisions in your life, do not beat yourself up. Learn to speak up and identify what exactly you have done wrong. After that, be humble enough to ask for forgiveness. Change yourself, and do not be too keen on changing others; they will not appreciate you. If they do not forgive you, it is not your problem. You have already done your part. If the other person chooses to remain angry with you, he or she will end up being an extremely bitter person, which leads to all kinds of stress and illnesses. Another important point is, do not jump to conclusions about other people. You are not a mind reader. You may think that the other person will never forgive you, but it may not be true. If the situation becomes worse after the apology, walk away. You have done your part.

Recognizing Guilt as a Poison and Laughter as the Best Medicine

I also learnt to laugh at myself at times, say, when I sing out of tune to myself and realize that I do not have a good memory for lyrics. I chuckle at times when I think about how cute my cat is—he is spoilt just like me. Many times, too, on the radio station, you hear others laugh and joke about things and situations around them, and you end up laughing with them. What a beautiful cycle of positivism! Pass it around, and it will never end. Sometimes if you get bored out of your mind, go out to a bookstore and pick up a comic book or something from the humour aisle. That will make your day.

Starting a Self-Smile Campaign

One time, as I was walking through a mall, a couple was just sitting down. We looked at each other and smiled. When you smile, the world smiles back at you. I was invited to sit down with them and have a nice long chat about their culture, and the good and happy times they had where they came from. On that day, I realized the importance of appreciating others' points of view and their own peculiar sense of humour. Each culture has its own. Open your eyes and you will realize the world is not just about you. If you have enough time and money, go to a comedy club; have a good laugh at some of the jokes. If your budget is tight, go on the Internet or watch a comedy on TV. That will also make your day. There are many ways to cheer yourself up when you are feeling down. One day, when I was feeling "blah" at home, I decided to push myself out to do some window-shopping. I put on my best dress and went around the mall. I was pushing my cart around, and I accidentally hit a little girl slightly in front of me. I felt so embarrassed, but the little toddler was so cute, and she didn't cry. Her mom picked her up and said very nicely to me, "It's all right . . . not a problem." Every little positive statement like that makes me happy within myself. I started to praise the little toddler for being such a good brave girl when she didn't cry. The mother's positive attitude made my day. When you apologize sincerely and smile, the world smiles back at you. I am an enthusiastic individual who delights not only in bettering myself, but in assisting others as well. This way, you will bring joy to many around you.

Realizing that Silence Is Golden

As much as we become occupied by the business of the day, there are many times when we all need to just be still and do nothing—that is, relax and spend moments of nothingness, with no problems on our mind. Hypnotize yourself by visualizing mountains, waterfalls, and beautiful flowers. When you reflect quietly on the beauty of the world, you will eventually feel the peace within yourself. Never hate to be alone. We need space from others to learn to be by ourselves. If your friends or colleagues cause you stress, when you get home, sit down comfortably on your chair or sofa, turn on the radio, and listen to favourite songs or classical music to soothe your nerves.

During my quiet moments, I discovered more hobbies. I had always loved journaling. This helped me as I wrote out all the disturbing events in my life, analysed whether they were worth dwelling on further, and, if not, made a change to improve the situation and not repeat the same mistakes again. It is by determination that we make positive changes in our lives, rather than moping on the negative things of the past. In your own mind, try to wipe the unhappy events into the sea of forgetfulness, and replace them with good memories of the past and the present. It is a complete lifestyle that one needs to address. This is your personal choice, your life; it depends on how you want to steer your own life toward the right direction. For all the negative statements you write in your journal, tear off those pages and burn them. Tell yourself that this will be the end of the negative past, it is burnt out of you.

Putting an End to Worrying

Stop worrying! Do not worry about tomorrow, for today has enough trouble or goodness, depending on how you look at things. Do you see the glass as half full or half empty? It is about perspective. During the times when you are well, write out as much as possible the strengths that you have, all the good points, hobbies, desires (within your financial budget), all your past achievements, no matter how big or small. Never think of yourself as a failure. If you do, you are just pushing this negative thought further into your mind. There are many times we do things in a subtle way that injures our own spirit. Our spirit eventually breaks, and we stress ourselves even further. What is the point of chastising yourself? Is it leading you to a proper pathway in your personal life?

You need to set boundaries for yourself in your thinking. Otherwise, how are you going to improve your situation? Much worrying will lead to further anxiety problems and panic attacks.

Say to yourself: not everything has to be perfect. No one does everything 100 percent! Do you know that many successful people in the world fail many times before they achieve excellent results? However, because of their determination not to allow worries about failure to rule their lives, they manage to get past the bad times, and in the end, they gain success. Stop abusing your mind, body, and spirit. There are things you can control within yourself; it is about self-acceptance. Build good self-esteem, set goals for yourself, develop good communication skills, be able to say "no," and learn to be assertive. It is all about acceptance of oneself and one's situation, changing oneself for the better, letting the past go, dealing with it, and moving on.

Pacing Yourself

We live in such a fast-paced society that we forget to slow ourselves down. Multitasking actually leads to many illnesses, thanks to the stress that we cause ourselves. Don't allow circumstances or others to boss you to the point that you cannot control the busy-ness of your own situation. When you get home, it will be very difficult to unwind and relax, and ultimately, it affects your sleep. A disrupted sleep pattern causes many more problems, including depression, which leads to hallucination, heart attack, stroke, cancer, and many other illnesses. Is this what you want out of life? Of course not. You need to nurture yourself.

One of the benefits of going to a Day Clinic program for outpatients was that I learnt about stress management via breathing techniques, light yoga, exercise, and tensing and releasing techniques. In a room full of people or even by yourself, you can take in a deep breath—feeling it down through your stomach—and then let it out slowly. Do this a few times. Light yoga is excellent; not only will it keep you fit, it will help you lose the weight gained from all the medication that causes water retention. Of course, you have to sweat it out. As for exercises, be careful: do not strain your back to the point that you hurt yourself, or even jog to the point that you hurt your knee joints when you get older. In everything you do, pace yourself. There is always a balance we all need to seek.

Improving Your Memory

Sometimes when people are extremely depressed, they suffer memory loss. Before it gets worse, before you panic and lose focus, write things down. Try your best to improve your concentration by reading, say, one sentence at a time if you don't understand it. I have gone through it all—even watching television, I did not get the gist of the content. This happens when I allow my depression to elevate to the point that I have to increase my medication. I am not saying that pills are not good, but if you can avoid putting yourself in such a situation, isn't it better? There have been many times I was heavily medicated to the point that I could not focus or read or understand what people were saying. In my mind, I kept thinking about my problems and was totally out of the world. This is a situation we all need to avoid. Trust me, when you get to this negative place, it will take a long time to get out of it.

I have been depending on pills all my life, but they affect my memory. Still, nothing is going to stop me from pursuing my dreams. I set goals for myself; this is where I find my inner self. I question myself. Do I want to stay this way and act like a vegetable, or be useful to myself and contribute to society? Maintenance is what I aim for. For example, since I have a bad memory, I needed a pillbox to remember what to take and when to take it. I make sure that I have an appointment book so I can write down the things I need to do for that day and the days after. During the year 2002, despite my illness, I was able to study while working full-time. I was able to obtain two A-pluses in Human Resources and one A in another class. I took pride in myself for my achievement. Now, taking pride in oneself does not mean boasting to others about yourself; otherwise, you will cause a whole lot of jealousy around you. From what I learnt, it is best to keep your mouth shut when it comes to your best achievements. Just pat yourself on the back and share with those who are really close to you. They will be happy for you as well. Meanwhile, you can encourage all your friends to do the same as you have done. This cycle of sharing your good thoughts with others will encourage your friends to know that there is no end to what they can do in life.

Managing Weight

Just recently, I read in an article that researchers have found pollution in the environment from lead and cadmium to be extremely high, and this has contributed to an increase in neurological disorders. It is, therefore, very important that we learn how to eat healthy and stay healthy. One of the side effects of medication is that it could lead to obesity, so one must focus on following a regimen of not eating higher than, for example, in my case, 1,200 calories. This is based on my body mass index or BMI (Keys 1972). This index measures the amount of fat in your body according to your weight and height. How do we count our calories? The answer to that is diligence in watching the labels on every item you buy from the grocery store. You may come across charts that show you how many calories vegetables have. If you are one of those who is extremely concerned about weight gain, seek a nutritionist.

Next point: exercise is of utmost importance to our lifestyle. You have to ask yourself, is it worth sitting on your couch and doing nothing and feeling bored? Idleness could also lead to too much thinking in a negative way as well. There is a time for everything. You have to try to push yourself to your limit to do light yoga, for example, if your health does not permit you to do a rigorous activity. Those who are able need to get out of their comfort zone, go for a marathon walk; and wear a hat and sun tan lotion if the sun is too strong, to protect them from getting skin cancer. There are many types of exercise. One may choose golfing, badminton, table tennis, tennis, sauna, swimming, cycling, or treadmill. If you are shy about going out, do your exercises from home. Buy yourself some weights, download exercise programs, study them, and do them when you can. You can even buy a low-cost DVD or video that shows different types of exercises. You can pick and choose whichever suits you. Note that it is vital to drink at least eight glasses of liquid as you exercise, particularly since some medication causes dry mouth.

Getting Enough Rest

As you have read during the first half of my book, my sleep was constantly affected. I either could not sleep at all, or I slept so much that I could hardly work at all. Therefore, finding your own ways of achieving your optimum level of sleep is important, including sleeping at the same time every night. Meditation is imperative too. The word *meditation* does not only mean prayers, although prayer plays a great part in my life. Meditation can be in the form of counting from 100 backward to one, or visualizing how beautiful the flowing waterfall is, or being in a forest or a beautiful bright flowery fairy-tale garden. Other ways of meditating could be reading until you fall asleep, or listening to soft quiet music. Tightening and loosening your arms, body, and legs is a good way to relax yourself for sleep.

Keeping a Budget

I realize that, being Bipolar, I have a tendency to want to spend lavishly on things that I don't need. I would even purchase coins advertised on the television and sponsor children when I was in a state of mania. I maxed out all my credit cards to the point that it took me about three years to pay it all off. I was fortunate that my parents and a friend helped me with it, together with an inheritance that I obtained from my relatives. These are the people I am very thankful for. Now I make sure that I stay within a budget; for example, if I have $1,200 for the month, I make sure that I can balance my account without overspending. Yes, it is tight for me, but I receive good things from the food bank, food vouchers from a church, and help from friends who treat me for lunch whenever they can. I am grateful to those people too.

Staying on Medication

After I graduated, I started a career in customer service at a vinyl company. I loved the job and my employers. Deep inside of me, I was extremely proud. In 1993, I had to move to another location and apply for a job closer to home. Within a week, I was hired. I had such a sense of achievement and pride that I decided to go off my pills, as some friends of mine were telling me that I should. I started listening to their advice, and that was my downfall. I was irritated when an ex-colleague of mine was sexually harassing me at one point. I flipped and yelled, and my anger was uncontrollable again. My boss, who liked me a lot, was really stuck in his position. At the same time, where I was working, other colleagues were bullying me too. I did not have the ability to be assertive; I became aggressive instead. *This is not the way to go, girl*, as I think to myself now. Sadly enough, I was let go despite the fact that my boss still appreciated my work, as I found out later on when I visited him and others. They were never angry with me; they soon found out what was wrong with me.

I mentioned to them, when I visited to apologize, that I tried to get off my pills on my own on a gradual basis. It was my mistake, and I can't blame anyone but me. As my doctor reminded me time and time again, I should never stop taking medication on my own, despite what others tell me. I may look good on the outside, but the synapses in my brain are not functioning properly. There is a chemical imbalance in my brain cells. I need the medication to balance my mood swings. It is difficult, as I have written from the beginning of the book. I had to be in the hospital for two months, subdued with five different medications. My friends were shocked to see my condition. I couldn't read, write, sing, or play the piano. Those were my dark days. Worse, I felt that I was gaining weight with all the medication, and I felt extremely ugly inside of me. This led to very low self-esteem. Even when others praised me for looking good on the outside, I never accepted their compliments, as I just didn't believe them. Please learn from my experience. Do not go off the medication on your own, or you may end up in the hospital for the longest time. You may constantly have attacks every year. Ask yourself, do you want to be negative in your thinking, which leads to unhappiness, or do you want to be a positive individual where nothing can stop you from attaining your goals?

Feeling Thankfulness and Gratitude

After years of suffering emotionally, I learnt a life lesson to be thankful and grateful to all my friends, doctors, nurses, relatives, and most of all, my parents, who have loved me the most. Recognizing every little blessing that comes your way from people who are kind to you is of utmost importance, so that you do not take things and people for granted. I remember Mom, especially, having to travel back and forth to support me. Dad had to sacrifice financially all his life to support us. Thinking back, if I didn't learn to be thankful, I would have time and time again failed to acknowledge those who helped me during my lifetime. I attribute my good upbringing to my parents; they taught me well in terms of morals and values that I am able to carry out now. Gratitude turns one around to be always humble. Many a time, I would seek to help others who fell in the same category as me when they cried, got upset, felt depressed . . . I just wanted to reach out to, basically, say to them all, "There is help, if only you seek it." We live in Canada, where the healthcare system is relatively good compared to many other places in the world. We are fortunate that the cost of going to the hospital and counselling here in Canada is relatively lower than most countries. Unfortunately, many are not diagnosed until it is too late; they break down and will not understand their situation. Hence, when you are successful in life, never look down on those who are sick and unable to work. You may end up the same way when you get older.

Having Faith

This is a topic that is very sensitive to some. However, there are many studies that demonstrate that when you have faith in God, somehow He carries you through. I will not elaborate on this too much here, but I will be writing more books to reach out to those who are interested in this topic. Faith is not about a specific religion. Faith is believing in Him who can carry you through all sorts of situation. It is trial, error, and tribulation that will build a stronger character in us. A stronger character will build perseverance and hope. Eventually, faith builds love, not only within yourself, but in others who fall in the same way you did. Faith and time will heal all wounds that have been inflicted on ourselves or each other. It is also important to learn forgiveness. If we do not forgive, we become embittered with people in our lives. Worst of all, we do damage to our own psyche. So what is the point of being angry with yourself and the world? As I have already pointed out, love actually covers a multitude of sins—negativity in one's life and others' as well. Love is all about self-respect. If you are happy within yourself, you can reach out to others with respect. This becomes a cycle of positivity, a merry-go-round, around the world and back to you! It is all about self-control. What part of that don't we understand? With self-control, one is able to strike a balance within oneself. *Mood swing* is a relative term to some, but to others, it is not easy to comprehend why we go from feeling extremely high to the opposite, which is depression. Even if you have the faith, God cannot help you if you can't help yourself, let alone others who may feel extremely burdened by your problems. That is why counselling with a therapist is very important, especially if you feel that medication is not your cup of tea. There is always a positive resolution to every problem. The challenge is, do you want to take the positive solutions or the problems with you throughout your whole lifetime?

In conclusion, my advice—not only to anyone who reads this, but to myself—is to learn from mistakes and choose not to repeat them again. There is definitely a light at the end of the tunnel if you persist by the power of your mind to think, speak, and act in a positive manner, not only to yourself but to others as well. It is obviously a matter of self-control. Do everything in moderation, and most of all, count your blessings. It is written in the Bible to love others as you love yourself. The question I have for you is this: how can you love others when you are not taking care of yourself? Pamper yourself by talking to you yourself gently. Be realistic about your situation. Do not worry, but focus on things that could uplift your mood. Hang in there when things get rough. Tell yourself it is mere transience, we are just passing through. Be resilient when bad things happen to you. Be strong within yourself to pull yourself out of any negativity. Just tell yourself that you will learn to be wiser in your life experiences. Grow and age gracefully. As Eleanor Roosevelt said, "No one can make you feel inferior without your consent."

There is a difference between and IQ and EQ. IQ tests are based on math, visual, verbal, reading, vocabulary, memory and spatial imagery. EQ—emotional intelligence—is about common sense, achieving your full potential, interacting well with others, keeping a positive attitude in life, and remaining highly flexible and adaptable, with good practical problem-solving skills. Value your own uniqueness and that of others. I would like to end my story by quoting this:

Proverbs 23:7:

"For as a man thinketh in his heart, so is he."

REFERENCES

Beck, Aaron T., A. John Rush, Brian F. Shaw, and Gary Emery. 1979. *Cognitive Therapy of Depression*. New York: The Guilford Press.

Bartlett John, 2002. Bartlett's Familiar Quotations 17th Edition, New York: Little Brown & Company

Burns, David, MD. 1980. *The Feeling Good Handbook*. New York: First Plume Printing.

Ronald Fieve, MD. 1989. Moodswing. New York: Bantam Books

WEBSITES

Access1: www.access1.ca

Canadian Mental Health Association: www.cmha.ca

Centre for Addiction and Mental Health: www. camh.ca

Community Resource Connections of Toronto: www.crct.org

COTA Health—ACT Team: www.cotahealth.ca

Hong Fook Mental Health Association: www.hongfook.ca

Pathways Physical Activity Programs/Minding Our Bodies: www.mindingourbodies.ca

The Scarborough Hospital—Community Day Clinic: www.tsh.to/pages/community-day-clinic